Rawshock

ALSO BY TOBY FITCH

Everyday Static
(Vagabond Press, 2010)

Rawshock

Toby Fitch

PUNCHER & WATTMANN POETRY

First published in 2012
Published by Puncher and Wattmann
PO Box 441
Glebe NSW 2037

http://www.puncherandwattmann.com

puncherandwattmann@bigpond.com

National Library of Australia
Cataloguing-in-Publication entry:

Fitch, Toby

Rawshock

ISBN 9781 921 450 617

I. Title.
A821.3

Cover design by Matthew Holt
Typeset by Chris Edwards using Monotype Apollo
Printed by McPhersons Printing Group

This project has been assisted by the Australian Government through the Australia Council, its arts funding and advisory body.

Australian Government

Australia | Council
for the Arts

"Off with his head!"

—THE RED QUEEN

Contents

Oscillations

Everyday Static

On the Slink

Bottles in gutters,
alley cats on the slink
            under streetlamps that crystallise
        in the corners of my eyes —
shopping trolleys gliding by
            like giant legless ice skates —

            this brittle night taken out of the fridge —
        it's spring but cold still,

            still as glass.

        Sobering up, a breeze —
    if I cast a rock up through the air,
            between the wires, the tooting owls,
                beyond the rooftops
    into the twisting funnel of stars —
                I could almost crack open the night

                and swig.

Tangents

A drive up the street is light, is a boon —
    is full of female matadors.

The moonbeam is a tangent
    glancing off his eye juice —

a turn of the head, a crick in the neck,
    tearing the muscle in his chest.

She's an epiphany — the fifth element
    setting off dominoes —

    prang after prang into prang
as reflectors sing the car-crash song

    and she flickers — a film projector
batting her eyelids at bull-bars

    like tremors after an earthquake,
tearing the chest muscles of other men

    (any man with a memory)
up and down the strip.

Beelines

Anyone with double vision
can tell why the small black dog

steers clear of astroturf;
why the dog's eyes follow magpies

that navigate via junctions;
why veering in squares, not circles,

the blue car makes a beeline
for a lamppost, the traffic light

goes gridlock-orange, a bullet train
is trapped on never-green tracks,

and jets fall out of a marooned sky;
why, on waking today, my vision stings

and my face is puffy: dreaming

is forced to move along paths
that are too well-paved.

I'll sleep with my eyes open,
stop my shadow running away.

Floe

In abeyance, the body sinks
into the weeds for weeks; the mote
doing roundabouts in the moat of the eye
ceases to trouble or seize the soul, flattened
like a rubber sole; deadened eyes
in headlights fade to dust as roadkill
reeks under tyre-tread; tired limbs in limbo,
flags that flop loosely in the wind; the faculties
lose their facility, nothing within arm's reach
or cheek by jowl; no howl from the invalid mouth
stuffed with one insipid mouse; the toes,
unable to tow the two, flat, pinned-
and-needled feet; too heavy like the brain
in a skull full of rain, an ocean liner
at the bottom of the world, wedged
in a fat ice floe.

Narrows

And then comes the morning when it dawns on you
the sun is not going to rise any more than you will
above yourself; when, in the midst of the mist,
blinkers have crept up the sides of your
cheeks, corridors have closed in like
garbage-tip walls, doors have
disappeared, and the past
repeats ad nauseum,
hissing from the
gutters like
steam.

You've awoken to dead-ends stacked up, like bodies en bloc,
no exit signs, no *wrong way turn back*, where gambler's
luck is never looking up, and if you're honest
no one's sure what you mean, where self-
abandonment is out of vogue, tunnel
vision is the new black, clouds
have descended so low that
even the supermarkets
are dark and everyone
is looking for some
way out, any way
out, not a mirror,
anything but
mirrors, just
a window
— open
to let
the
day
in.

Fluff

Milling about the city's nightlife,
she threads through the quilted crowd
who rug themselves up, flattering
each others' leathers and wispy flair.
She stands on the fringe like a lost
strand of hair, listening to the needles,
the knit-knot words, the pinning-up of
phrases — cottoning on to their lingo.
She's ready to be brushed aside
when some guy's quip poufs her up
like a pillow, though she responds by
chewing a ball of fluff because, for
some fuzzy reason, she wants his hide,
sewing what's left of her heart to
her sleeve — a threadbare cliché
that his quiff-like puns pierce
like a pin-cushion. With conversation
wearing thin, his hand reaching for
her velvet, she remembers the lint
piling up in the corners of her
apartment; the frayed curtains she's
never closed on her view of the city.
She can see it now from her bedroom
window: the silhouetted skyline, a
tattered hem; the stars, little white
cross-stitches forming a sky of blind
eyes; and rolling over Centrepoint,
the moon, a silver ball of wool,
unravelling.

Aubade

In sticky haze under dappling trees,
   shadows and limelight
      coagulate
  after coalescing
     through the night.
Emerging to a lurid sun
     that slides up into the deep,
   lifting its crusty eyelid,
      I walk
  down a pointless thoroughfare
    of morning people,
      dumb pets
   and coffee.
The stale alcohol
  and cigarette breath,
    the scintillating light
  and compression of garbage
have a Doppler effect
     on my stagger
      so I skip,
but no matter how fast I skip
     away from sidelong glances,
     round corners,
   under shopfronts,
impersonating shadows
      to outfox the light,
  I can't escape the smell
     catching up with me
  of someone else
     on my skin.

Parallels

The intervals between trains are shrinking,
streetlights quivering —
one or two blink out
with every repercussion.

Planes fly lower and lower,
guard dogs whimper, and
every so often
a seismograph flutters

as if to warn us
that the orbits are out of whack,
that waves rake the ocean floors
and the hairs on the backs of cats

stand on end
because something unparalleled
is about to happen.
Light a candle, stock the cupboard —

alarms and sirens
have cancelled the silence.
Pay no attention to screams or the jitters —
when someone bolts, everyone bolts.

Whatever you say, say nothing —
as a bystander
amongst the panic and the vomit,
do nothing and nothing will bend.

Poles

The weft of future rain
whets the windscreen.
Pulled ahead,
sliding from pole
to pole,
almost a head-
on pile-up,
the slippery eel
of a wheel fights
the fate of travel,
wipers trawl travail
and, in a second
so swift a swerve
could go either way,
the coupé sideswipes
oncoming traffic —
tyres having come
terrifically unstuck
from tar that never
tires of sticking it
to the terrified,
the fatigued,
the tipsy
and the turvy,
the heft of
future
rain.

Spine

Dazed
and mute,
calm as a monk
above the city
din below,
a cigarette butt
swirling
thru a vortex
of coruscating
reflections,
black blood
bottled up, he
steps to the edge,
silent as snow,
and jumps,
his hair a wisp
of wind,
buffeting shirt
a cloud, eye
twinkling,
mouth a black
hole, a vacuum,
sucking in the air
to bring back
the words, bring
back the world,
until he connects,
spine first,
a match sparking
bumper-to-bumper
with a car's
windscreen.

Twirl

If
we were
to fling our plans
up into a whirring fan, we
might take a turn for the worse or,
at the least, slam into the wall and flop
to the floor, tiny yellow birds twirling our
heads. And to rub our throbbing-red
noses in the dirt, we might
look back beyond the
propellers in the
waves and
murmur, "we were,
we were …" instead of
casting a lighter spin on things
and chuckling, "we whirr, we whirr…"
like the quirky few, who find unknowingly
that the fan is the ultimate reflection in
the lagoon, where sunlit raindrops
fall circles-in-circles and life
is all children, arms out
and spinning fast till
the last fall down
into dizzy
deliri-
um.

Relapse

Think of stagnancy, think fog,
and the libido reels into the bog;
the psyche drives in drivel; wheels
of reflection roll backwards, running
on rubato; a slow-burn heat in the head,
the heart creaks like a handbrake, sinks,
breaks on the creek bed of the gut; clutched,
in a rut, bubbles rise, reflux; sex drifts like
a flaccid fish in a plastic bag; lungs collapse
in a hot lap dance, refrigerated for years, icebergs
accumulating tears from a young age gone under
in rumination; ribcage like a used shopping trolley
drooping from water under the bridge; duped
by mud, Echo in mind, a blind apparition
lapping in the mire.

Sonar

From a drunken cruise on the harbour
comes a bouncing melody: *I wanna
have sex on the beach*. You can

see it on everyone's (anyone's)
mind as the summertime trees nod assent
in the Botanic Gardens,

their scent wafting up to the nostrils
of skyscrapers breathing in fumes,
pumping out bucks,

relaying UV to the ant-sized joggers
who bound up and down along the shoreline
on sand grains jostling for legroom.

Above them, birds, checking out the goods
of a small grey woman staring at the bridge,
thinking: *I wanna walk across water*

like sound, as her skin remembers a distant
prickling, another season,
a sun and a wind that lifts her hairs.

The Race Home

Flying rats have hijacked Hyde
Park. Under straining winds
and the flare of a low sun, grey
suits peck at each other,

buses keel over, school kids learn
new words to mouth off;
the homeless feeding the birds are
incensed by a hunger not their own.

Yet when the sun parks down
between scrapers, there is a lull
as inflamed heads cool off
and a boy and his beagle, Jekyll,

send the grey blanket of pigeons
fluttering across the orange glare
in a crosshatch of rapid eclipses,
mini and various.

Centrifugal

When tar gets in the gaps
b'tween words, words
b'come targets for bulldozers …
snap-easy, flattened-
out small-talk … 'tsall torque
and no talk, reheating
in the microwave, the change-
rattle of the exchange,
melting, chitchat churning
in a talk-torpor, our
cement-mixer mouths, so-
as-not to dry up like
snot … what'sa matter with
things without matter,
if the snooze-button's there
to warm us up, if we're
still asleep, zap-numb in da
evening, wadching re-
dundant washing-machine
dreams … if things wid-
out madder get fladder, never
dhinking why, just wai-
ding for dhings and microwave
dings, wha madder?

Mannequins

If we don't move, no one will
see us. The air-con will help us

to lean forward, help us to make
headway. Regular news updates

from dozens of flat screens
could save us from our musing as

blow-dryer music in the hi-fi section
warms the backs of our necks.

If we stand anaesthetised by the
cleaning lady's spray gun,

dressed in the latest, we might blend in,
and late at night, when we're blind,

security guards will make love to us,
though only with their torches.

In the corners of the ceiling, next
to the cameras, radiant silver vents

will inhale our carbon dioxide, while
the vents along the skirting boards

exhale, to keep it circulating, this
air we breathe on condition.

Blackout

At some point, the power went out.
You thought you'd left your appliance

on too long, or the gin was wearing off.
Still, you felt your way down the

stairwell of vanishing spirits
to see what all the din was about,

passing from inner blackness into the
deeper blank of the inner west,

and still couldn't see it, whizzing past
your ears, nor the clear, high-beam

eyes of the local wildlife that'd crept
down eucalypts, across dewy grass

to stop at the gaps in the fences.
The animals could see it, though:

you, turned to stone, your kids
swinging from the power-lines,

and the atmosphere, alive
with evaporating sparks.

Library Animals

(after Shakespeare)

She leads me up
to the eighth floor of the library
where eerie dust,

shushed by a coy
draught, kindles
amongst the shelves.

We snake in and out
of the aisles, looking for a corner
or a space as dark

as a room in bedlam for us
to become the rude myth
of our birthright.

But with no Venus glove
for entering the nest
of the phoenix

we're both fair game.
And the idea of it, of flesh,
almost becomes an impediment:

the spiced rivers of her hair
in our lips as we kiss;
the knuckles of her spine

like the rivets in her dress —
obstructions, abstractions, words
in the way — that is

until our burning will touches
the metallic shelves
like lava meeting glacier,

bumping the goose
in both of us,
steaming up the windows

that turn a blinkered eye
to the odds of being caught
red-handed.

"Put some more English on it,"
she whispers, with
my finger on her forepart,

as unbridled, I risk the faux
pun: "Are you a woman
given to lie ...?"

But that's not
how she does it now, alive
in the dusky back

passages of the library,
where the dimmed fluoro
and deep shadow

bisect our civil demeanours,
where we succumb at last
to our lower halves,

making love like centaurs,
a discreet but riveting
performance

to a hushed and studied audience
of thousands laid
before us in many positions,

though mainly standing up
and jacketless, front
to back.

Everyday Static

Driving along alone
between unforgiving buildings,
raindrops flicked up by tyres,
airwaves breaking

like rain on a windscreen,

reminded me of you and me
in the car, in static:
windscreen wipers tired;
the tyres flat;

the fire and its mountain-flames

hovering in our minds
like a back-seat driver gone to sleep;
the world at water level as we pulled up
and gazed out into the harbour,

mountains and rain dissolving in lumpy waves.

Winded on a Trampoline

I clutch at clouds,
burn my brow on sunbeams,
lick blue moons with a rainbow scythe.

But as day caves away
a wind whips through my stomach
and I'm dumped in its wake.

Magpies brush low over cut grass.

Thrumming cicadas numb the wet sandstone.

A pair of sneakers over power-lines.

Purple and gold in the clouds above.

Some stars beginning to stir.

Cavernous

He used to tell me the strangest things,
like how there are spiders
in the wind that comes from the sea —
a wind that tunnels through
homes, cars and towers,
hollowing them out.
It's hard to argue with him
in the shadows of these cliffs
facing the ocean,
the top-heavy overhangs
reaching for the sea,
the wind-carved caves
of pale grey honeycomb —
spider webs
spun with stone.
Beware of Falling Rocks
says a sign that creaks
as the wind ups the tempo
of its whistling, eating the land
as only the air can.
And rocks can be heard
glunking into water
like creatures from beneath, or
scuttling in the shadows of the cliffs —
now shadows of their former selves.
It's hard to argue with him in this
darkness between immensities —
in the face of the ocean,
back to the world,
the wind filling in
what has been carved out.

Reaching Out

You can wait
like a great sad wolf
for the moon to rise,
or you can launch yourself flat
across the sky:
a pebble released
from fingers
to skip across waves,
clear the jagged white tips
of a shark mouth,
turn the tides
drunk
on aquamarine wine,
gawk at the beauty
Andromeda
chained to a rock,
spit, scream,
vomit,
whatever it takes
to tear off that carcass
of a shell,
slip through
Poseidon's
falling trident and
wonder at your wake
as you scale the ocean's abyss,
soar up, above,
beyond the last port of call
and leave behind
a thousand thoughts,
a hundred hearts,
ten nicknames,

six degrees,
skim one
last,
two last,
three lonely skims,
countless in all,
to the cold horizon
before succumbing
to the gulp
of salt,
a pebble sinking
just short
of the pink
sunset.

Rawshock

*"When Orpheus descends to Eurydice,
art is the power that causes the night to open."*

—MAURICE BLANCHOT,
from 'The Gaze of Orpheus'

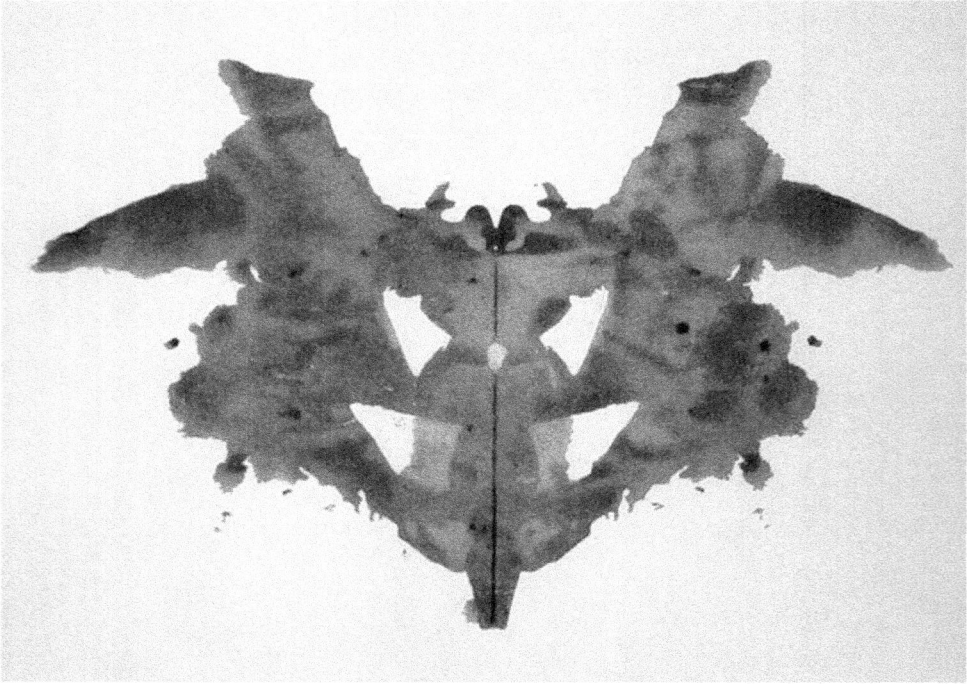

I

O   E
Orph   e's not
an ortho   dox liar,
replete with his   newly   high-strung lyre
in the shape of a moth, or pelvis. His pincers thrum my box
as we coalesce with our big bad wolf masks on, yowling at the sky,
watching each   other morph   in the storm
clouds, in the stains   on our   bed sheets: a pair
of bats twirling thru   the smoke   of a fallen city. Pity:
despirit despite my spooky resemblance to purity, E perfect
I prefer   the white lies,   the chase,
the dis   placement of   his face
when E remind him I'm not
quite the damsel in
distress, O
no
\ /

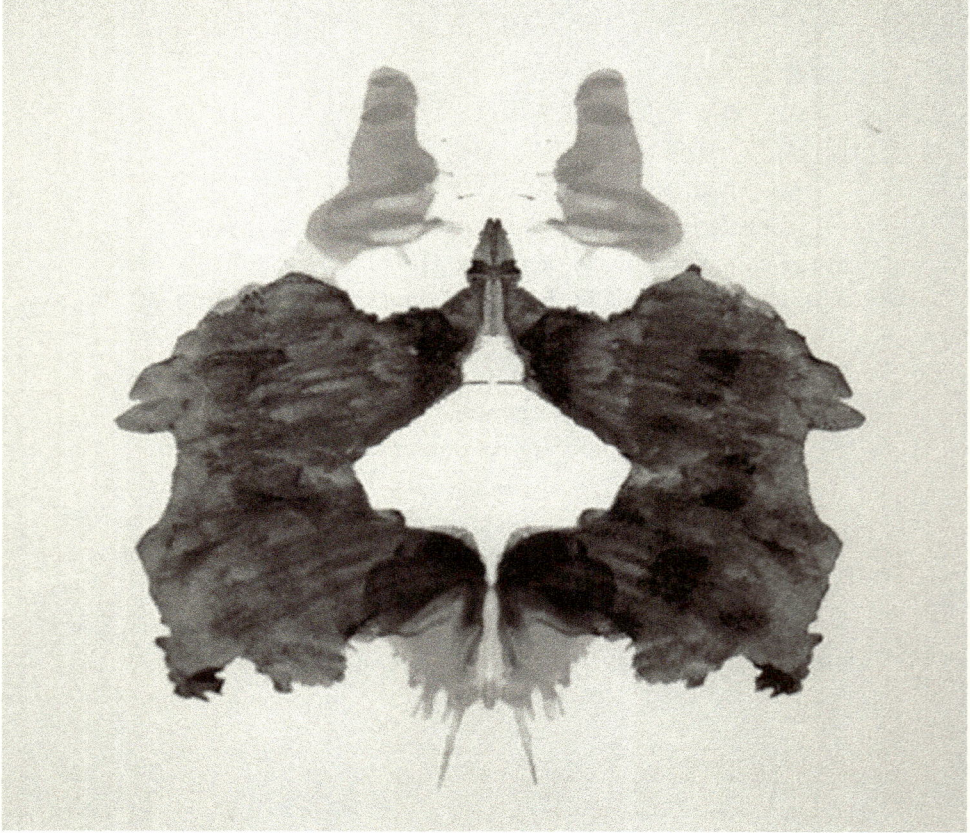

2

H   H
Ha   Ho
How g   loomy.
In this m   meadow,
A
we have   nothing   to lose
but our sense of   adhesion, and B,
we didn't have much   of   that to begin with.
Glue me to your wedding gown, E, the night is upon
us. Your white beauty   sits   unwitting on my lap
as bloody acrimony   sssnakes its melody
ssmoke around   your canklessss
sssssssssssss   sssssssssssss.
I want my sssshh   ssshhadow back:
where's our pre-nup I sing and bite, come
back to us Bacchus, come back! But the
ocean ebbs away C you in the sHades'
b e a u t y
/ \
/   \

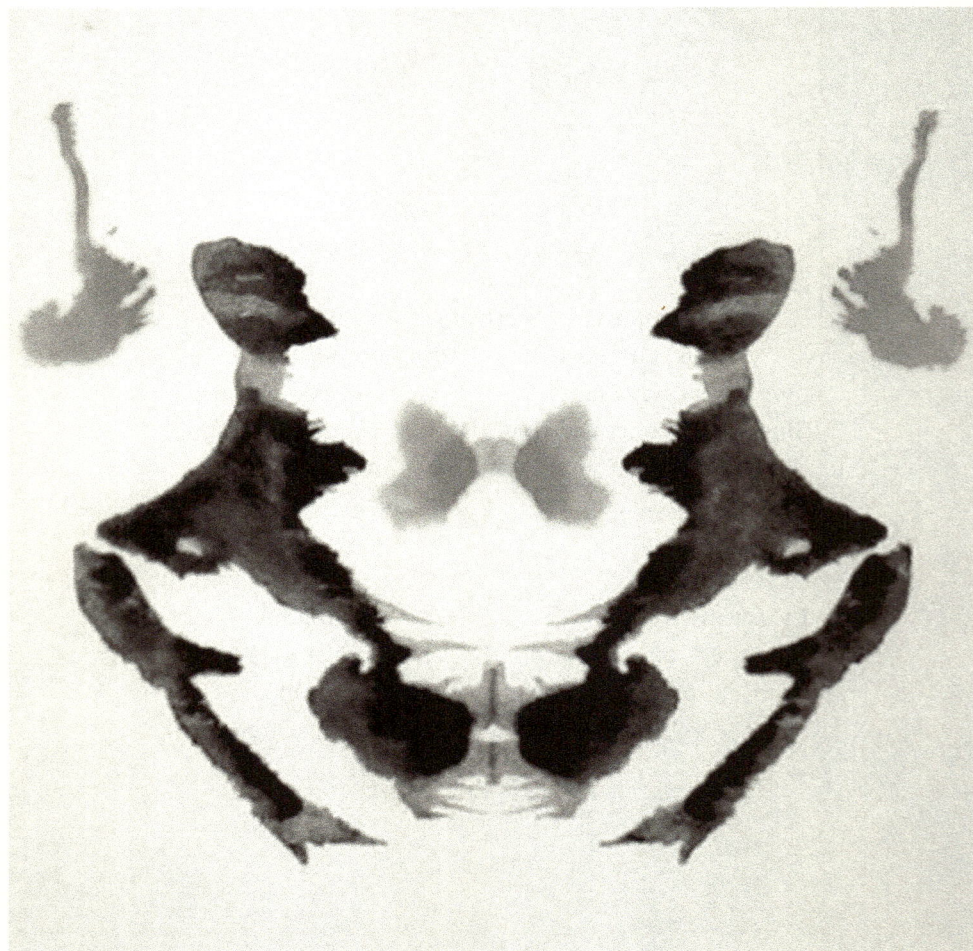

```
y                                                                                a
 y                                                                               a
 y                                                                               a
 you                                                                            bat
  bit me      Bbaaaa                                    aaaatt!    outta
"like          Blue lyrics                           hack us a        hell."
                part again                           and this
                 time it's                           terminal.
                 ———                                    ———

                 ———                                    ———

         The fuselage      ( 2 he  arts )      comes away
       from its red wings.     ) bleep (     O said nothing is
      certain, E, spinning    ( as n    one )      the moon on his
  finger,  lifting orchids                        in the air, but now
          the memory                            of E's voice
descends          thru an                  upside        down lake
 of clouds             to the               under              belly
 of the                world,             where           vultures
     gnaw livers      and  a man       pushes the     weight of his
       suicide      up a hill.  Am   E  deaf,  like after     sex, or
        in a             coma? It dœsn't matter as            the
         wreck           age slows to a crawl.       E can
           fin              ally hear my            self
              think                          think
```

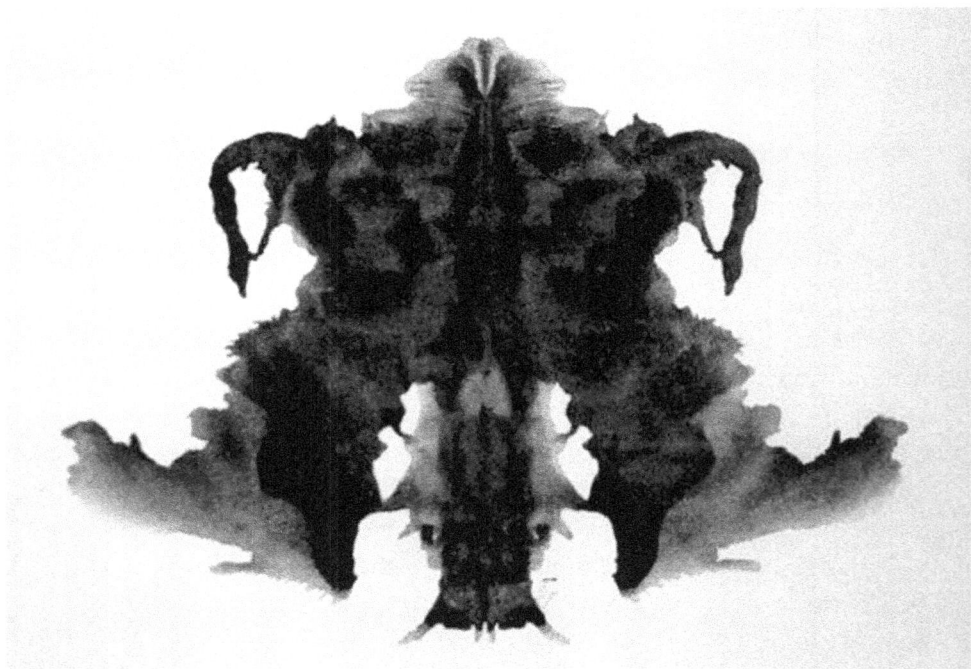

4

O U
can collide
with a bus "in error",
hold schrapnel and rocks aloft on your way
((down to Erebus. You can seduce the   ))
(ferryman, queen Persephone, have   )
(the fatty-fat, serpent-backed   )
Cerberus melt in your palm,
caress his moth-eaten earlobes
as the Furies   snivel   at your feet,
stop Sisyphus   in his tracks,   Ixion's wheel,
Nyx   and the Styx   as stoned   as onyx. You   caN
collude   with Chaos   all you like,   but you can't   waive
the fact like   my father   Apollo did:
E don't   need to   follow
t h e   s u n

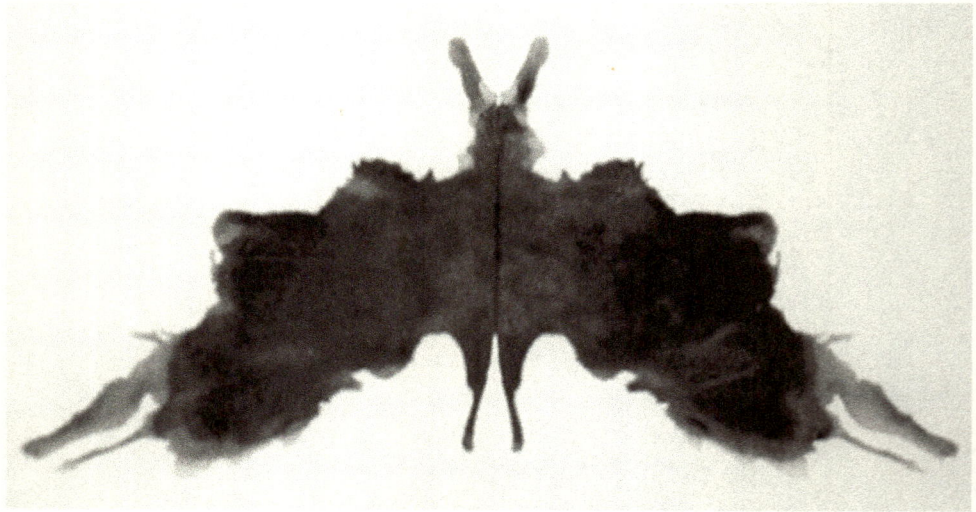

     !   !

     o   e

    œ œ

    Gimme

more   Nec   tar &

Ambrosia! Skull the ether! Cut me out o this

chrysalis   so I can sing of asterisms winking

& dice rolling, so I can wing it thru buildings

like a lunar scythe.   Fal lin'   from obscure dés

astre, O've got the taste   e o   for star-blood: stick it

in ma   gaping   ! !   operatic   maw.

6

On
our
wa way up to to
th the he
top
past
welled-up
b   roots of blood   d
through the forest of mist O planted
in our minds, and the crowds of
ghosts running smoke-fingers
down our spines, up gnarly
cliffs of barley black and red
unruly spider lilies, over bridges
spanning the void, on up through
the great blind lake condensing across our faces,
sensitive and invisible, electric and invincible,
on our long way to the top
all O can think of is
laying her out and down
on an ani   mal rug.

7

<pre>
        i   i
       Ni   ght
       is   so
      bri   ttle
  e c l i p ti c   & w h i t e.
     O don't   E know
   w h e r e   t o l o o k
o'er-exposed,   drenched in
   milk. Sink   ing thru
   depth of   sky-field
    as bright   U-bombs
        dis   em
         bowel the un   der gro und,
      the pinpoint of night opening to
     capture "it's curtains" on film, I gaze
         at U. The rest is a daze, is
            hissstory. E lip tic.
</pre>

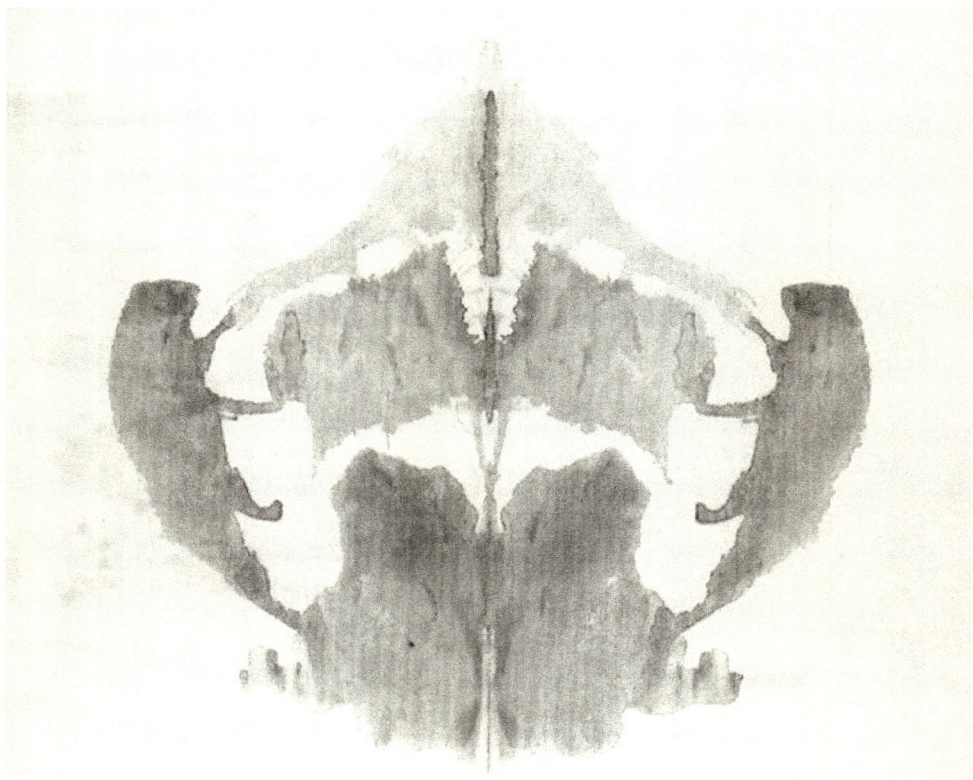

8

                                    Œ
                                  It was
                               then that E
                            walked up beside you
                    e   Orpheus.   o
            i   — u —   i
  we)   We were two — — pink panthers   (ha
slinking   up through — — the dappling   shade
(inking   up up thru — app appling   Hades).
And E could   feel your ribcage blue   and green
  pulsing   like a   \ /   reptile's   heart,
   cold,   \/   could
   feel the   fire under | foot, and I   told you
      o u   not to look at me.   o u
            o   Not because   u
                    I didn't want to go back
                 but because E thought that was
                      what   you   wanted.

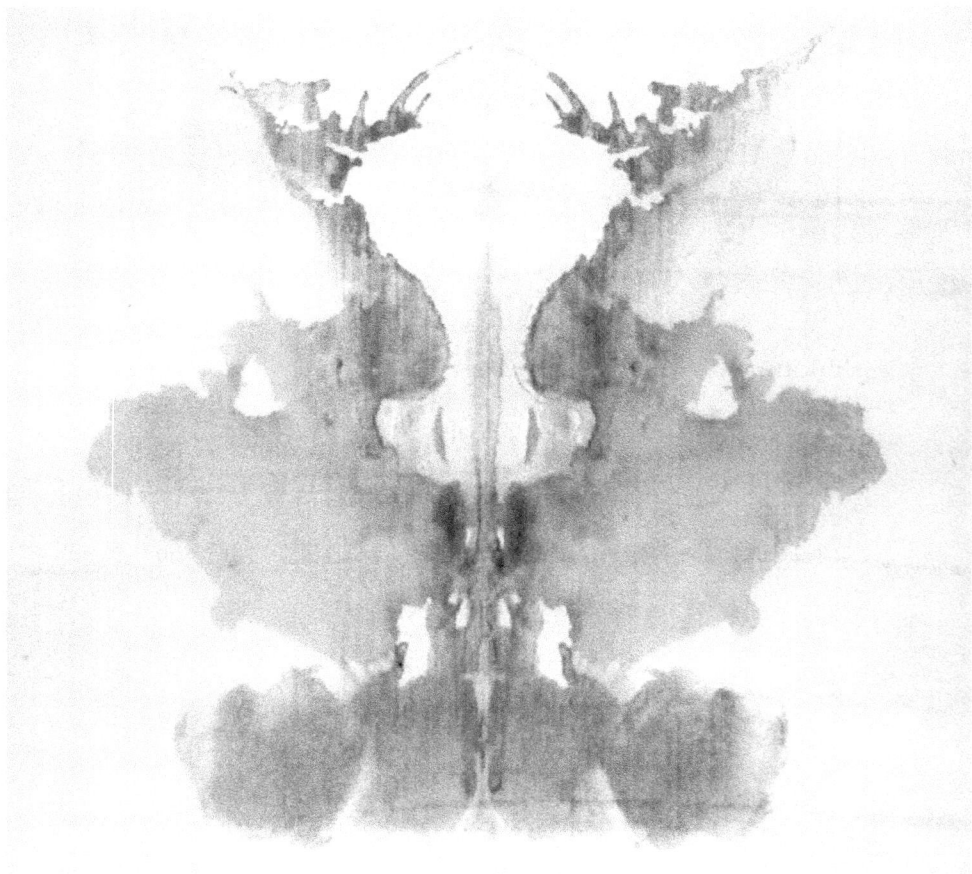

9

y y

y y y y g y

y e l w w l o w

o oud ( ) sky e

Orph-cloud sssky-bruise

before y ou could

ssslip awayy

sslip away

I saw you in the) (lake's reflection,

i saw you in the lake's reflectio n,

amorphous O cloud stalking the last light

wreath-like, eluding ( ) the clutches of dusk.

wraith-like, illusion of the coming dust.

Before you were lost to me, wolfed by the

Before you were last to leave, wolfed

by the) black (bonfire

lake (i r e) sky

the lake caught you sipping the sky

smuggling a draught a raft of blue

into into Stygian Stygian daylight.

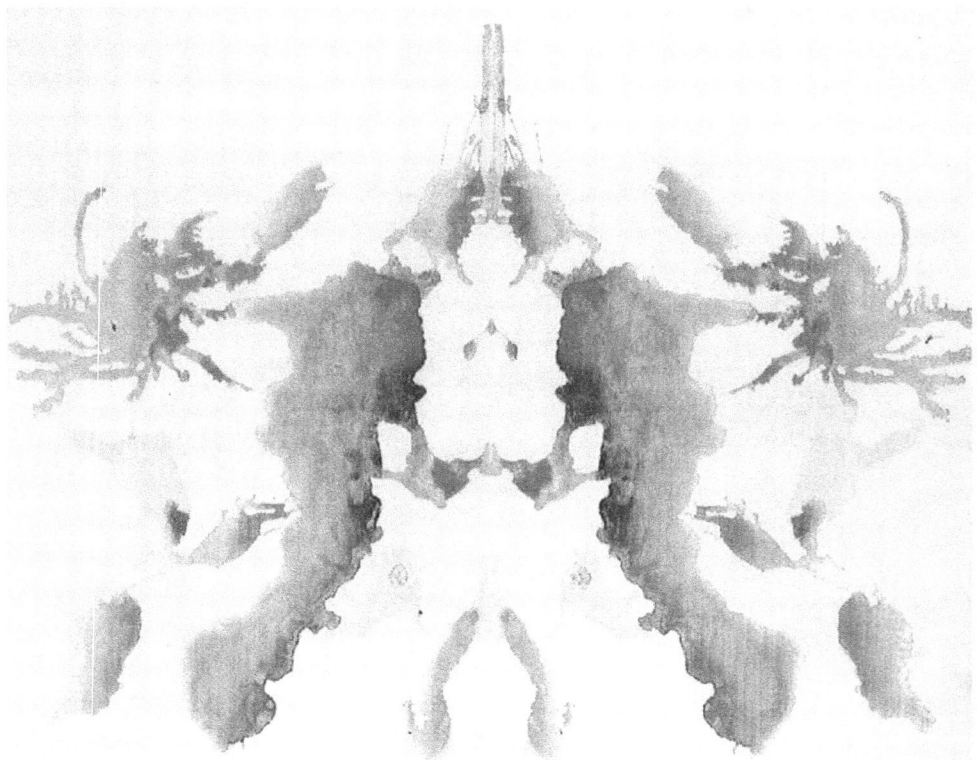

```
                              !!
                              !!
                              S
                              ad
            s                 and                  m
    (               a         unbridled        a              )
    (    s   S   d        m e r c u r i a l,  m a d      d      S   t   )
P     s    e           possessed    b   y     nothing            r   i    P
  o     s        but art, stripped            by drunk women      s    p
e    s    d        of all I took        a     for granted.        s    d     e
  d     o      o      Bones &      a   a       borders       e    i    d
                     countries                 comfort
    z  Z          mean zip    to        i     me   now, the         Z   z
       i       sparkling dawn trickling all hell & high water         o
       p    s   down my        thr     oat,      my limbs   e      n
         s s     strewn acr                    oss earth.       e e
                  Shipwreck   ed              in    oblivion
                  pulsing anci ent      t      riv ers through
    d          my veins,            th         Eurydice,            o
    n        I can turn             t h e                trees inside     u
    a        out, O am           the    flo             wer fields            t
               & the               sun     blu              sky.
```

Oscillations

Apnoea

Last night I lay awake
  in bed, listening to the house
and planets whispering.
  I fidgeted and they fell silent.
The universe swept itself
  under the carpet,
darkness overflowed the bath: I'd
  upset the rhythm of things.
    As I held my breath,
  the nocturnal sighing
returned: a poltergeist
  began humming in the attic,
swinging his hips to the pulse
  of the southern lights; a possum
shook comets from a canopy;
  hooping winds bundled the moon
through my bedroom door as eerie creatures
  from the neighbours' pipe dreams slid
like liquid sugar down the alleys,
  kissing the streetlights out with enormous lips,
and I promised not to make a scene again.
  I lay awake, motionless and soundproof,
as the gutters creaked, the tiles cracked,
  and the windows crystallised,
waiting for the stars to breathe out
  and space to unfold.

The River Seine

(after Paul Celan)

Tonight of no stars, only clouds —
a city wrapped in crumpled paperbag.

The cigarette, a cork in your mouth
like traffic in a bottleneck

longing to get out.

You can see the horn-sounds
as colour above the river.

This dark-houred clock, your flawless water,
will only embrace the open ones —

those who've thrown a stone in their eye
and felt a ripple from the pupil out.

So in hesitant hope
your cigarette smokes a thought … 'rebel'.

But to turn this world to verb —

to hurl yourself in the river
and feel the razor-tooth skeleton bite.

No, something invisible
has summoned the wind

to warp the word into 'sober'.

O all this hoarded time
gluing elbows to our sides.

Only semi-submerged, barnacles
have formed on the bottom of our souls —

words not worth uttering anymore.

Our reckless abandon is derelict
with insouciant desires.

To turn this world to verb, get a life …
No, not to go out like a firework,

red flower in wilted sky —

to pitch yourself in the river like a stone,
disintegrate and drift,

wash your mouth out in the ocean
where sea-wave and sea-roar,

ssssshhhhh —

even in a whisper
will never cease trying to shut us up,

though we're saying nothing really at all.

To stub out your cigarette on the vertical stone
and sink into the river unnoticed …

O in the deep upon deep
comes the caesura —

the break between worlds.

Orbits

(after a line by Prévert)

This money that rolls
that doesn't stop rolling,
stock market blackouts
and bigwigs purring, cars inter-
secting, generations over
-lapping, bungled-up bank accounts
from slow-colliding satellites,
a break-up in static, snowballs in the air-
waves as a world
-wide tide nibbles away
at coastlines,
gulping little souls on lunch-
break, running from an overheated
greenhouse into the red,
run into the ground by imps,
their spastic euros, dispensed
from plastic trees, fluctuating in the air
-con, impulsively combusting in record time,
please sign on the dotted line ...

while outside, an unmanned unicycle drifts by

and all the gulls,
even the ones that aren't hungry,
fly upside down and in circles, green-
backed by green spotlights
that hypnotize the blank-cheque sky.

Emotion Sickness

All wobbly all over —
    it's not so much vertigo
        as an aversion to inversion. Carry on
            kidding yourself it's giddiness,
                the bluff of your blood-
                    flow; some old neophobia.
                That carrion you
                    forget to keep in mind, i.e.
                the equation to your qualm, may be
            in remembering the moment
        of your memory,
    however fractured that keepsake
has become — the closer
    to broken the better though,
        and confronting it by
            donning a monocle helps
                to make the ground
                    seem farther afield.
                        No need to be stable to drink
                            at this oblique
                            table. In oblivion
                            it's easier being queasy any-
                        way, and damn near
                    impossible to assure
                that certain bleak hauntings won't
            see you stepping ashore, upside-
                down the morning after,
                    a black-and-blue sea
                        hung over
                            the world.

Finding H

(after Rimbaud)

To find my imagined girl
   on the other side of the globe,
I erected trees on every corner,
   hung silver chains from windows
to branches, red lights
   from main drags to summits,
cabled oceans to clouds and stretched
   a golden, interweaving
net of orbs over the continents
   to link our distant cities together.
I stood on a mountain with my tablet
   downloading the seasons
and spun from newfangled spinnerets
   a pop song with themes and variations
to raunch the riverbeds, undulate concrete
   and shepherd the galaxy
     into a single omniscient cloud.
And I streamed it to everyone!
   I taught the world how to search for love
through a screen, without leaving home,
   their points of view at one remove,
     icon to graphic icon.
That's how I found my imagined girl;
   she sits in my study now, rapt
in a torrent, tormenting the swivel chair.
   Through the keyhole I can hear her
surfing my precious web, pressing
   her own buttons.

La Fée Verte

(after a line by Apollinaire)

My glass has shattered like a burst of laughter,
   pale green light sprinkling rain.
Seasick flowers bloom through the floor
   while across the room
lips of a steamy creature fall
   agape, her eyes grinning in my direction,
     blonde hair awash.
   O fey licorice, paregoric
of my second childhood, ease the pain —
   take me to the cloudburst
     and the gushing of her name.
   I can see my reflection
in the blurred Van Gogh to the left
     but that's not the liquidation I seek.
Not even the sugar and ice I spill
   down her cleavage can make up for it.
     Take me away! What has been seen
   cannot be unseen (the cameras
will babble and froth come morn,
   hail or shine), so when I'm asked to leave
     I stand up and pass out
   into the street — heavy-headed tulips
brushing against my shins.

Le Pont Neuf

Romantics, werewolves, lunatics —
eat your hearts out!
So cries the city, pretty night-
lights twinkling.
There's a full moon rising
and a king tide to boot,
but just try footing it
from your better half
on Pont Neuf ...
Forget it, cobbler —
the bridge is in love
with a deep-rooted fairytale
and won't let go; having
survived the revolution,
the World Wars,
she's unlikely to crumble
in the frigid drizzle that's
tenderly embraced you
in its clutch. Zut! — she's
got you by the goolies
and wants another kiss ...
Paris is howling! — even
the moon is puking its delight!

Blockbuster

Out
of the river
comes a hulk of a thing,
pulling itself up with the utmost
grace by bending bridges like gymnastics
bars — a wet coat on a hanger. How toxins
glow on its viscous shoulders — neon syrup
meeting the smog-clouds and dragging them down
by the ears as if to say *you're in on this too*, this shift
in matter. It oozes between the city's monuments like a
slow tsunami yet to climax in whitewash, and just as it
clicks with the viewers, who consider an exodus, the
sun comes out, mooning and starring in a last-ditch
effort to engross. The cashed-up hand of god —
here comes the dénouement — feels up the
audience with the speed of light, venturing
like a leviathan to spawn maelstroms
but fizzling off-screen, a
snail in its own
goop.

Critical Mass

The buses, hippos and whales know what I'm wading through,
shouldering clouds of quicksand, swayed by pressure — these
crates of cortisol I've ordered en masse. Blue in the face, on all
fours under the ice, I must be the obese star of a B-grade blue
movie!

       OK, maybe my seriousness is getting the better of me,
but nothing

compares to this elephantine ocean. Ugh, what a body of stodge,
impenetrable, even for something as lite as the hackneyed light.
It takes an aeon to shift position, get comfortable, let alone
create a wave in this fishbowl full of glue.

The Living Daylights

I wasn't always larger than life. Once, I was merely a slight disturbance, shaking idle office blocks, steaming up the windows like some tiny bull in a china shop. The neighbours called the cops once their crystal started rattling, so I rose through the pipes, shed my lack of thorns, set my sights on gnarlier heights. Later, I descended, too: at fancy joints and filthy dives, I blew out foundations, blew away dust. Gripping my first tower felt like strangling a giraffe, but I soon took shape, gathering speed and diameter like a runaway boulder, sharpening these new earth-shattering powers of mine to the point where butchers' knives feel blunt. As a demo in a control lab, a model in miniature of the havoc I mean to wreak, a bursting mirror-ball might seem apt, but my parallactic gift is now more jagged than an ice age, more deafening than mosquitoes in the dark, as clean-sweeping as a tidal wave, bloodier than raining frogs. It's something King Kong would have been proud of. Scatterbrained Orpheus can look back over his shoulder, but where on earth will he find the love to look up, at this? My glittering terror of a rainbow: so purely see-through, yet capable of knifing concrete; so inescapably eclipsing, prismatic, tongue-twisting, there's no point running. It's ten times more blinding than a meteor under a magni-fying glass. *Shard-fall*, is what I'll call it, or maybe

shattered *rain.*

Dry, Mainly Sunny

For those of us left behind
on Earth, autumn has devolved into

scrap-heaps; the oceans have mostly
transpired. No one remembers exactly

when dry ice began to fall on this
no-man's land where sleep is

barren, geography redundant,
history blotted out, where

huge insects and deep-sea creatures
wage war in surround sound,

bombarding each other with black
holes and white dwarves

while we mutate below —
our haven a heaving underworld

from which the lucrative few take off
in their pleasure craft, their hyperbole,

in search of greener planets. What we know
's contrived — channelled, naturally, down

thru the digital feed, with the marketing
snuff, hoodwinking anyone

cranked up on dark matter, or hooked
on live bulletins — terrorism as

prime-time sport, talking
heads popping each other off —

schrapnel and tits the memorabilia for sale
on a website designed to look like

a crumbling art museum. One click links you
to a pornsite of the gods where Zeus,

the Minotaur and Madonna coexist and love
lingers as a computer virus,

a glitch in the mainframe that you,
babe, with your trigger finger

glued to the gaming console, drift off with
into cloud-fracking cuckoo land, free

radicals running amok, your dreams in
bits and pieces, in compromising positions,

emulating the projections of the divine
plasmas that dance, ecstatic,

on the cave walls around us. Look! —
Our children's children, stick-figure monsters,

are throwing shapes and grinning like roadkill.
They flicker, they rally in vain, for who

-ever's held at ransom in these pixelated,
shade-haunted, red-carpeted jaws of

hell-bending doublespeak. A wag's tongue
somewhere is tickling the multi-coloured

drips of fat, the blips and bleeps, and
the coffee-stained corpse in the fridge

is getting nostalgic for what that glitch
in the system felt like, or for some other

feel-good story. Such divinations
are loony tunes to the beaming prophets

who've evolved into our puppets —
their gravitas is ancient string

theory, bankrolled by the gods
for spoon-feeding the not-knowing

what they're saying when they say
we are resuming normal programming:

your forecast for today is dry, mainly
sunny, but tomorrow will bring a spell

of rain coming in from the east,
and the west, which will continue

at least until the weekend.

Inter Alios

(after Aeschylus)

We fall
for each others' / clashing
colours / orbit
each heart / drunk & adored / libation
bearing all / sneak
up on each other / aloof but obsessed w/
enigmas beneath the skin
imbrue and invade / brood then turn pink as it
brews within us / the way a
glass of milk turns / a single drop of blood
into an ambulance spinning / en
route to a mop-up / curdling in the grave
we inter each other in turn
in / alien / suffused /
swooning

Irritations

I plant forests, and they wither
                    behind me. There's a traffic light

in my heart. Which colour? I don't know.
                    The high-pitched whine circling my head

isn't a vulture, it's my halo. My double haunts me
                    in windows and lakes; the size of his eyes

erodes my mettle. Wherever I travel, metal
                    detectors go mental and the stink of burnt

sugar stalks me — crackling, always crackling. When I
                    fuck, my mind drifts. My whores

say it's a lack of friction. I guess I'm made
                    of cold blood, my skull is full of earwigs, my

visions littered with wheezing stars:
                    in the mirrors on the ceiling, miracles

have ceased. I blunder across these bitter
                    nebulae, hemlock on my tongue — no wonder

I've got the sniffles! Only a nightmare
                    will help me sleep tonight.

Dyslexic

Who would've   thought that at
  birth, my double-helix world would be dropped

    on its head — that it would spiral on its mis-
      informed axis into grand self-delusions

      — upside-down, dyslexic! What an ex-
        panse of nothing — what an ego

          standing on its head, looking
          down at the sky, the abyss

            — cities like stalactites,
            elevators to the tips.

        I drop my lot out the windows,
        watch it plummet into space — take

      out birds along the way to the cosmic
      pits. The poles will capsize (or right them-

    selves, who knows?) — so to breathe in the
  auroras orbiting the meridians, I hang myself from

  lightning conductors like a big, red, weighted balloon
awaiting my   last breath.

Tennis Court Pantoum

What had you been thinking about
I thought going down to mail this
I go on loving you like water
All the way through fog and drizzle

I thought going down to mail this
There was no turning back
Through fog and drizzle
You were not elected president

There was no turning back
Toward the corner of the wall
You were not elected president
The blood shifted you know

Toward the corner of the wall
What had you been thinking about
The blood shifted you know
I go on loving you like water

While We Were Dreaming

A million vehicles came and left the metropolis

Hairs tumbled onto shoulders

A corner shop was held up at gunpoint

A southerly buster swept across the mountains

Sets of keys and lyrics were forgotten

Countless amateur videos were shared, downloaded

Someone's cancer found its own cure:

Eurydice, discovered by a blind musician

Your other half pondered infidelity more than once

My doppelgänger dove from a pier

Marquees were assembled

A hand unfurled

A lily in the sun

Forty thousand fans went silent at full-time

Two strangers made love in a cubicle

Kids drank from goon bags

Held each other's hair back

A bouquet of balloons snuck across the horizon

Massive rocks moved within the earth

Twilight got invaded by stars

We seeped into each other's sleep, tidal

Oscillations

Attracted to all things electrical, you passed along the way like a weird
storm then returned, waxing lyrical about your adventures: the glow-
worms that lit up the tropics like guide-lights on a runway; dinosaurs
grumbling in their graves; the plethora of cats that scattered when
you moonlighted as a monsoon. And what about those ant-sized,
funny-looking apes pointing up, fawning over your tresses (like
twisters they'd seen on TV)? Magical spices from across the
way incensed a certain inability to stay put — the pull of
turquoise oceans, and vermillion clouds yet to unsettle.
You left me in your wake: cities of electrons leapt from
state to state, erasing to-do lists; umbrellas lifted off;
thunderbirds and fossils quivered at your flights of
fancy dancing on their arrivals boards. I could feel
a tremor whenever you kissed another, the great
bite of opposing time zones, but no — the lure
of a new language, the smell of grass, dirt and
rain, foraging for alchemy or hang-gliding w/
juvy dragons — you came to pine for a less
personal kind of love, an ascetic on snow-
caps where landslides of quartz fell deep
through deserted lakes. After a disserta-
tion from a nomad who'd hobnobbed
with the gods, you split the atom with
a lightning rod looted from Olympic
towers — rainbows and whirlpools
erupted in the sky! It was a fitting
salute. Now here you are on my
doorstep, my old dog Cerberus
humping your leg, here you are,
replete with impulse purchases…
though who'd begrudge you the
souvenirs: a leviathan in a tea-

cup, a snow globe of the Sahara,
various trinkets from the Under-
world. Love, since you vaporized,
a cosmic war has given the stars
the creeps, I lapsed with an old
flame, the water's been unsea-
sonably luke — I swim in vol-
canoes so my flesh can sting
like it used to. I thought you
were a myth, that the pictures
of the back of your head, sent
from distant photo-booths,
were some kind of cruel
joke. What a ruse! Remind
me never to look your way
again. Argh, scratch that:
before you vanish over
the horizon, can we ar-
range to bump into each
other at the equinox,
the southern cross or
the northern auroras,
unrepentant, on the off-
chance we might earth
each other once and
for all? or will you
pass along the way
again like a weird
storm, with a wink
and a wry smile —
lightning striking
root through
stone, the sea
going down
with the sun,

fire falling
back into
things
— the
planet
chang-
ing
sh-
ape
in
yo-
ur
e-
y-
e
?

Junction

(after Reverdy)

To pull up
    at the lights,
        yield my shadow
           to the sun,
                lean back on the wave
                and take the lip
                for a pillow…
                    Or to pull up and hesitate,
                    amber lights
                    filling my eyes
                    till my head's a
                  haunted house,
                till the wheel like water
                  escapes through my fingers…
              And I continue, wavering
          till the dawn beyond the final night,
      traffic piled up in the rearview
    mirror like a whitewash of words,
none of which can tell me the right way.

The only way to cap
off the night
is to decapitate yourself. The
clouds are out of reach
so lose your head to the bottle, art,
virtue — bottoms up!
Forget how your shoes melted near
the sun. There's
always a new pair at the grog-shop
across the street,
beyond the black river, beyond the
brake-lights, I
click-clack your toes, awaken the
spirit of Hermes,
step into the flow — steering
clear of cops,
their bright-dead eyes
impaired
by the dusk —
wing it
to the other side
on the
wind, a wave,
a star,
whatever!

tcap

                              Looking back over
                          the river
                      (or was it a pond?), we see
                    your reflection —
                a teetering kid with a crumpled
               paper boat floating
             behind the surface. You could almost
           leap over it but
         I'm lazy, so you slide through
        the portal
      without touching the sides, slip
     through the cracks,
      becoming luminous — a dipsomaniac
     at one with the
     green fairy, genie above the battle,
      mage of the
      imaginal — your breathing,
       your body,
      our day, uncorked like a
     bottle rocket
    scotching the lime-
    light. Now
   feel the fabric
  of the
 clouds.

Citations

'**Library Animals**' gleans words and images from two Shakespeare lexicons found in Sydney University's Fisher Library, one on his animal imagery, the other on his sexual word usage.

'**Rawshock**' reshapes the Orpheus and Eurydice myth using the ten original Rorschach inkblots as templates. The poem appropriates phrases from poems by Arthur Rimbaud, Charles Baudelaire, Stéphane Mallarmé and Rainer Maria Rilke. The imaginary speakers of the poem take the parts of Eurydice and Orpheus thusly: E, O, E, E, O, O, O, E, E, O.

'**The River Seine**' includes phrases inspired by the poems of Paul Celan, a German-language poet who committed suicide in 1970 by drowning himself in Paris's River Seine.

'**Orbits**' begins with the last two lines of Jacques Prévert's poem 'At the Florist's', as translated by Lawrence Ferlinghetti.

'**Finding H**' paraphrases one of Rimbaud's 'Fragments' from Folio 12 and plays on his poem 'H'.

'**La Fée Verte**', 'The Green Fairy' — also known as absinthe. The poem begins with Peter Dale's translation of a line from Apollinaire's 'Rhenish Night'. The last two lines are adapted from a conversation with Oscar Wilde recounted in *Absinthe: History in a Bottle*.

'**Le Pont Neuf**', 'The New Bridge', is now the oldest standing bridge spanning the River Seine in Paris. It is known as a meeting place for lovers.

'**Dry, Mainly Sunny**' gleans a few phrases from the secret booklet hidden under the CD tray of Radiohead's *Kid A* album.

'**Inter Alios**' takes a tissue of an idea from Aeschylus's *The Libation Bearers*, the second play in his trilogy, the *Oresteia*.

'**Tennis Court Pantoum**' is decked out exclusively in lines from John Ashbery's poem 'The Tennis Court Oath'.

'**Junction**' is a re-visioning of Pierre Reverdy's poem 'Carrefour', or 'Crossroad'.

'**Nightcap**' hijacks images and phrases from Charles Baudelaire's poem 'Get Drunk' and Arthur Rimbaud's poems 'The Drunken Boat' and 'Genie'.

Acknowledgments

Thanks to the editors of the print, television and online forums in which earlier versions of some of these poems first appeared: *Aesthetica Creative Works Annual 2011*, *Australian Book Review*, *Best Australian Poems 2011* (ed. John Tranter, Black Inc.), *Drunken Boat*, *The Fish Anthology 2010*, *fourW twenty two*, *Literature & Aesthetics*, *Mascara Literary Review*, *Meanjin*, meanjin.com.au, *Nine Tenths Below* (UTS Writers Anthology 2005), *otoliths*, *Overland*, *Paradise Anthology 2011*, redroomcompany.org, snorkel.org.au, *Southerly*, *Space*, *The Sun Herald*, *Swamp*, *The Sydney Morning Herald*, *Visible Ink*, *The Weekend Australian*, and *Wordshed*, a television program produced by The Red Room Company.

Some of these poems also appeared in the limited edition chapbook *Everyday Static* (Vagabond Press, Rare Objects Series No. 52, 2010).

'Rawshock', the poem, was published online by *Meanjin* (March 2012) and as a folio by *Drunken Boat* for their Handmade/Homemade themed quarterly (NY: March 2012).

'Library Animals' was commissioned by the Red Room Company as part of a 'Stacks' workshop and featured in the pop-up book and animation *The Analogue Crusader*, by Tasman Munro.

'Oscillations' was shortlisted for the Peter Porter Poetry Prize 2012; 'While We Were Dreaming' was highly commended in the Vera Newsom Poetry Award 2011; 'Beelines' was highly commended in the Reason-Brisbane Poetry Prize 2010; 'On the Slink' was a finalist in the Aesthetica Creative Works Competition 2010; and 'Apnoea', previously 'Last Night I Lay Awake', was a runner-up in the Fish Publishing International Poetry Competition 2010.

Thanks to Judith Beveridge, Michael Brennan, David Brooks, Stuart Cooke, Michael Farrell, Robert Gray, Martin Harrison and David Musgrave for their advice on reading earlier versions of this book, or selections from it. Thanks especially to Chris Edwards and Frances Simmons for their endurance in reading multiple versions, and for their unwavering love and support. Thanks above all to my parents, Jaqui and Simon, for their love and encouragement along the way.

This collection is dedicated to small black dogs everywhere.

tobyfitch.blogspot.com